6. Pray for  help
in order to understand wh ılm
119:18 would be an appro to
God in prayer.

7. *Class teac* *course for group*
study will find some helpful suggestions on page 47.

how to
take the self-check tests

Each lesson is concluded with a test designed to help you
evaluate what you have learned.

1. Review the lesson carefully in the light of
the self-check test questions.

2. If there are any questions in the self-check
test you cannot answer, perhaps you have written into your
lesson the wrong answer from your Bible. Go over your work
carefully to make sure you have filled in the blanks correctly.

3. When you think you are ready to take the
self-check test, do so without looking up the answers.

4. Check your answers to the self-check test
carefully with the answer key given on page 48.

5. If you have any questions wrong, your
answer key will tell you where to find the correct answer in
your lesson. Go back and locate the right answers. Learn by
your mistakes!

apply
what you have learned
to your own life

In this connection, read carefully JAMES 1:22-25. It is only
as you apply your lessons to your own life that you will
really grow in grace and increase in the knowledge of God.

1

INTRODUCTION TO I CORINTHIANS

The writer

The apostle Paul (cf. 1:1; 3:4; 3:22; 16:21).

The date

This epistle is dated from A.D. 54 to 59, but the spring of 56 is perhaps correct.

The place

Written from Ephesus.

The occasion and purpose

This epistle was written on the apostle's third missionary journey in answer to a letter of inquiry from Corinth concerning marriage and the eating of meats offered to idols. Paul's first visit to Corinth had been the climax of his second missionary journey in which he had planted the gospel in Europe (Acts 18:1-18).

One must note the simplicity of his preaching at Corinth as compared with the type of message he had given at Athens. At Corinth the power of the cross was the whole message and did not have the philosophical arguments or elaborate controversy.

The Corinthian church

The Corinthian church was predominantly Gentile and had elements of rich, poor, educated, and ignorant. This church was troubled with cliques, and there was an element of emotional people whose extremes degenerated into immorality. The loose habits of heathenism clung to many. Yet Paul addresses such a group as "the church of God . . . called to be saints . . . sanctified in Christ Jesus" (1:2). He sought to meet their need by appealing to their high position in Christ and the reality of their union with Him. He then exhorted them to bring their spiritual state into conformity to their exalted standing in Christ.

Outline

Divisions—Corrected by the Cross

1:1-31

The believer's position in Christ 1:1-9

Before dealing with the problems in the Corinthian church, the apostle reminds the believers of their position in Christ.

1. How are these believers addressed?

1:2 _____

2. What has happened for the one who is "in Christ Jesus"?

1:30 _____

The weakest believer is *sanctified* (set apart unto God), for his heavenly standing is in Christ alone. However, the apostle proceeds to rebuke these believers for their *unsaintliness*. Growth in grace is progressive sanctification—becoming more completely "set apart."

3. What may God have to do to promote our sanctification?

11:32 _____

4. What is the purpose of these chastenings?

HEBREWS 12:10 _____

5. What important characteristics did Paul commend in the Corinthians before he turned the searchlight on them?

1:5, 6 _____

4

6. Generally speaking, how were the Corinthian Christians regarded as to spiritual gifts?

1:7 _____

7. In what belief were they especially strong?

1:7; compare TITUS 2:13 _____

8. What is said concerning their position in Christ?

1:8; compare PHILIPPIANS 1:6 _____

9. Who is our Guarantee?

EPHESIANS 1:13, 14 _____

The word *seal* signifies a finished transaction as well as security and ownership. The word *earnest* means a token or pledge that the full amount will be subsequently paid. Thus, the Holy Spirit Himself is our security that we will receive full salvation.

10. Since the believer's standing depends wholly on the merits of Christ, what must be the end?

1:8; compare COLOSSIANS 1:22 _____

11. While the Christian is often found unfaithful, how is God described?

1:9; compare I PETER 1:5 _____

Paul here follows his usual method of showing that when believers realize what salvation means, they will begin to walk worthy of the gift. Now he turns to the problem of division in the Corinthian church.

Division by exalting human leaders   1:10-17

12. How does Paul describe the problem of this early church?

1:10, 11; compare PSALM 133:1 _____

13. What is the only basis of true unity in the church, even though minor differences of opinion may necessarily exist?

JOHN 13:34, 35 _____

14. What is often the cause of division?

1:12, 13 _____

Note Paul's method of curing division by directing every eye to the Saviour. Christ cannot be divided, and He is the one center and source of spiritual unity.

15. What is the only kind of oneness for which Christ prayed?

JOHN 17:21, 23 _____

16. For what purpose was Paul sent forth?

1:17 _____

Paul does not minimize baptism, for he uses it to explain spiritual truth (ROMANS 6). However, he does emphasize his mission and thereby makes their division groundless.

Division by exalting human wisdom   1:18-31

In this section, the apostle shows the contrast between the wisdom that has its source in man and that which has its source in God.

17. How does the unsaved man with his pride of intellect regard spiritual truth?

1:18; compare 2:14 _____

18. Despite such scoffings, what satisfying answer will one find by accepting Jesus Christ?

1:18; compare ROMANS 1:16 _____

19. While men may express their ignorance of God in scientific terms, what do they have in the end?

1:19, 20; compare MATTHEW 11:25 _____

20. What is the only rock of true wisdom?

ISAIAH 44:24, 25; 55:8, 9 _____

21. Which doctrine lays open the depravity of the human heart and the insufficiency of man to save himself?

1:23; 2:2; compare Isaiah 53:5, 6; John 1:29 _____

_____

That which the worldly wise calls "foolish"—the preaching of Christ crucified and salvation through His sacrifice—becomes the highest wisdom to the believer (1:24).

22. Why can the born-again Christian praise God for the constant weakness which causes him to depend on Christ?

1:27 _____

23. In spite of the criticism of the world, what things does God use for the good of men and His own glory?

1:27, 28 _____

In verse 28 the word rendered "base" means "low-born," and the word for "despised" means "reckoned of no account." God makes use of those reckoned of no account and hopeless by the wise of this world, for the accomplishment of great purposes.

24. When God is at work through men, what one thing is certain?

1:29 _____

The apostle now reminds them of the position which the believer has in Christ.

25. When one has Christ as the source and condition of life, what has he gained as to standing with God?

1:30 _____

26. Since Christ was made sin for us, what are we made through acceptance of Him?

II Corinthians 5:20, 21 _____

27. What then is the only boasting an enlightened Christian can do?

1:31; compare Galatians 6:14 _____

7

You have just studied some important truths about divisions in the Corinthian church. Review your study by rereading the questions and your written answers. If you wish, you may use the self-check test as an aid in reviewing your lesson. If you are not sure of an answer, reread the Scripture portion given to see if you can find the answer. Then take this test to see how well you understand important truths you have studied.

In the right-hand margin write "True" or "False" after each of the following statements.

1. All believers are sanctified. _____

2. The chastening of God is to make us holy. _____

3. The Corinthian church denied the return of Christ. _____

4. The Holy Spirit is our Guarantee that we will receive full salvation. _____

5. Paul's purpose was to baptize believers. _____

6. The wisdom of God convicts and confounds the wisdom of men. _____

7. God may use the insignificant things of this world for His glory. _____

8. It is because of our ability that we will glory in Christ's presence. _____

9. It is through Christ alone that we are counted righteous. _____

10. A Christian should glory only in the Lord. _____

Turn to page 64 and check your answers.

True Wisdom— Imparted by the Spirit

2:1—3:4

Divine revelation and human wisdom contrasted
    2:1-8

We have just seen that God is able to use our weakness and our strength, our ignorance and our knowledge. The apostle now proceeds to note interesting contrasts between the natural and the spiritual, the world and the Spirit, materialism and spirituality, human wisdom and divine.

1. What should be the heart and purpose of all effective gospel preaching?

2:1; compare ISAIAH 8:20 _____

2. In light of the stigma attached to execution by crucifixion at that time, what remarkable decision did Paul make?

2:2 _____

3. How did Peter define the heart of the gospel?

I PETER 2:24 _____

4. What was Paul's estimate of himself in light of preaching such a gospel?

2:3; compare II CORINTHIANS 10:10 _____

5. Upon what did the apostle depend for results?

2:4 _____

6. Since there is no foolishness under heaven that has not been put forth in the name of "scholarship," how should the message of salvation be verified?

2:5 _____

7. How much of the deep things of God can be expounded to mature believers?

2:6; compare 2:10 _____

The word for "perfect" means "full grown, mature." One translation: "We have a wisdom which we utter among those that are full grown." Verse 7 is literally, "We speak God's wisdom in a secret hidden for long but now revealed." He is speaking, of course, of the redemptive purpose in Christ.

8. How is Christ described when He was crucified?

2:8 _____

Spiritual illumination 2:9—3:4

Now that the two kinds of wisdom, human and divine, have been contrasted, the process whereby divine wisdom is understood is discussed next.

9. What is the reason many untutored people are regarded as spiritually wiser and more powerful with God than many who hold scholastic degrees?

2:9 _____

10. By whom does God manifest Himself?

2:10 _____

In the original there is no adjective in the last phrase of verse 10. It is simply "the deeps of God." One may feel very inadequate when it comes to spiritual "deeds." "Thou hast nothing to draw with, and the well is deep" (JOHN 4:11), but when the Holy Spirit begins to give illumination, we begin to exclaim: "O the depth of the riches both of the wisdom and knowledge of God!" (ROMANS 11:33).

11. While worldly knowledge is taken in through the use of merely human faculties, how does one gain spiritual knowledge?

2:11 _____

All believers do not have the same degree of discernment. This depends on the habits of the soul, the study of spiritual things, one's watchfulness against sin, his faithfulness in prayer, and especially his habit of living with reference to the truth he has already perceived.

12. What did Paul firmly believe as to the source of his message?

2:12 _____

13. What happens to one's vocabulary after he has come to know the Lord and has studied God's Word?

2:13 _____

The last phrase of verse 13 may be translated, "combining spiritual things with spiritual words." The Bible-enlightened Christian will have a Spirit-controlled utterance as well as Spirit-controlled thoughts. We are now made aware of God's threefold division of the human family: the "natural man" (2:14); the "spiritual man" (2:15, 16); and the "carnal or fleshly man" (3:1-4).

14. Regardless of how complete an unsaved person may be in the natural faculties of mind, why are spiritual truths as a foreign language to him?

2:14 _____

15. What is the real difficulty?

JUDE 19 _____

The word sensual in this verse is the same as "natural" in 2:14.

16. What does spiritual truth sound like to the unregenerate man?

2:14; compare 1:18 _____

11

17. How much spiritual truth does the spiritual man have the capacity to understand?

2:15 _____

The word for "judgeth" means "examines." The regenerate person has all his natural faculties, but they are quickened by the Holy Spirit. Ordinary knowledge is as much in his reach as that of anyone else, but he has a depth of understanding which only the Spirit of God can impart. He has understanding in the spiritual realm where the unregenerate is entirely limited.

Verse 16 is a quotation from ISAIAH 40:13 and the word *mind* is substituted for the word *Spirit*. It could be rendered, "For who hath known the Spirit of the Lord, that he may instruct him? But we have the Spirit of Christ." Thus, the spiritual Christian has the capacity to know all divine truth because he possesses 'the Holy Spirit. This is the secret of spiritual illumination.

Although there is a chapter division, the apostle continues with God's threefold classification of the human family.

18. How does Paul describe these carnal Christians?

3:1 _____

The word *carnal* means "fleshly" and thus the reason for carnality is submission to the flesh, the old nature, instead of to the Spirit of God.

19. Why are these Christians babies?

3:2; compare I PETER 2:2 _____

20. What are some of the manifestations of carnal Christians?

3:3 _____

21. How was carnality displayed at Corinth?

3:4 _____

22. What then is the remedy for carnality in the Christian life?

ROMANS 6:13; compare GALATIANS 5:16 _____

---

check-up time No. 2

You have just studied some important truths about the true wisdom of God. Review your study by rereading the questions and your written answers. If you wish, you may use the self-check test as an aid in reviewing your lesson. If you are not sure of an answer, reread the Scripture portion given to see if you can find the answer. Then take this test to see how well you understand important truths you have studied.

In the right-hand margin write "True" or "False" after each of the following statements.

1. The purpose of effective preaching is to declare the testimony of God. _____

2. The apostle depended on his own ability and cleverness for results. _____

3. It is the ministry of the Holy Spirit to enlighten the understanding of Christians. _____

4. Spiritual truth changes the vocabulary of Christians. _____

5. The natural man has the Spirit of God. _____

6. Spiritual truth is foolishness to the natural man. _____

7. Spiritual believers have the capacity to know all spiritual truth. _____

8. A carnal man is an unsaved man. _____

9. The difference between a carnal man and a spiritual man is spiritual growth. _____

10. The remedy for carnality is to be controlled by the Spirit of God. _____

Turn to page 64 and check your answers.

Service and Servants

3:5—4:21

After dealing with the message Christians are to receive, the apostle next discusses the manner in which they are to work. However, the basic principle is the same. As the message is from God, the work is by servants of God in service for God.

Christian service 3:5-23

1. Who does the work, though through human instruments?

3:7 _____

2. As Christians, with whom do we labor?

3:9; compare 15:58 _____

In verse 10 Paul shows that the responsibility of the laborer is limited to the kind of material he brings into the superstructure which rests upon the Foundation, Jesus Christ. Moffatt translates verse 11: "The Foundation is laid—Jesus Christ, and no man can lay any other."

3. What vital instruction should be given every person who takes Christ as his Foundation and builds thereon?

3:10 _____

4. Noting the six kinds of material mentioned in verse 12, into what two classes would you divide them as to their enduring qualities?

3:12 _____

5. What happens to the value of wood, hay and stubble if exposed to fire?

3:13 _____

6. Describe the effect of fire upon gold, silver or precious stones.

3:13 _____

7. What will be the basis of reward?

3:13 _____

8. What is the purpose of this testing fire?

3:14 _____

_____

9. Since a Christian's faith rests in Christ as his Foundation, what about his salvation?

3:15; compare JOHN 3:18; JOHN 5:24 _____

_____

10. How are the good deeds of unsaved people described?

HEBREWS 9:14 _____

Whatever the good works of the unsaved, they lack the vitality which only the Holy Spirit can give. The vitalized works that merit reward in heaven flow only from the implanted life built upon Christ as the eternal Foundation (GALATIANS 5:22, 23).

In I CORINTHIANS 3:16 Paul reverts to the Corinthians themselves in a collective sense. Since as a body they were supposed to be a shrine for God's indwelling, they should see the gross impropriety of certain conditions tolerated in their midst.

11. How is the figure of a temple used in relation to the individual believer?

I CORINTHIANS 6:19 _____

12. How is it used here in the collective sense?

3:16; compare I PETER 2:5 _____

13. What happened to the Aaronic priests if they violated the sanctity of God's meeting place?

EXODUS 28:43 _____

14. What of those who violate the spiritual sanctity of the Body of Christ, as by false teaching, immorality, etc.?

3:17 _____

The word for "destroy" means "put out of commission." It is a serious thing to take part in anything which encourages a real breaking up of the union of a body of believers.

15. What is God's verdict for those who think beyond His Word?

3:20 _____

There are three appeals to believers based on the thought of the body as God's temple. (1) Since we are God's temple, guard against carnal defilement (I CORINTHIANS 3:16). (2) Since we are God's temple, seek for separation from the world (II CORINTHIANS 6:16). (3) Since we are God's temple, glorify God in it for it is His (I CORINTHIANS 6:19, 20).

Christian servants 4:1-21

We have seen Paul's opposition to all tendencies to worship man or for the servant's of Christ to keep pre-eminence for themselves. The apostle here continues the discussion of the place of the Christian servant.

16. How are ministers described?

4:1 _____

The word for "minister" used here is one that means "an underoarsman" or subordinate. A "steward" is one in a position of trust to another in order to use his belongings for the purpose agreed upon (LUKE 12:42).

17. What is the greatest thing that can be said of a steward?

4:2 _____

18. In the final analysis, to whom did Paul feel he was responsible?

4:4 _____

19. What warning does he give as to premature judgments?

4:5 _____

Paul is dealing with those who were perpetually sitting in judgment upon the motives of others, while failing to judge themselves (ROMANS 14:12, 13).

20. What is the tendency when teachers begin to go beyond the lines laid down in Scripture?

4:6 _____

21. Of what does Paul remind those who were assuming superiority because of their infatuation for some teacher?

4:7 _____

By contrasting their spirit with the experience of the apostles, Paul shows up the pettiness of their rivalries.

22. According to the world's standards, how did the apostles expect to be regarded for standing for the truth as revealed to them by the Holy Spirit?

4:10, 11 _____

23. How may one who stands high in God's book of estimates be described by the wise of this world?

4:13 _____

24. In spite of this, what should give the Christian confidence?

4:19, 20 _____

There are plenty of religious leaders today who are multiplying words to the fascination of multitudes, but they are not revealing the power of God. The true gospel message, regardless of how humble the messenger, proves itself adequate to overcome all the natural enmity of the human heart and make virtue attainable through the power of the Holy Spirit.

check-up time No. 3

You have just studied some important truths about Christian service and Christian servants. Review your study by rereading the questions and your written answers. If you wish, you may use the self-check test as an aid in reviewing your lesson. If you are not sure of an answer, reread the Scripture portion given to see if you can find the answer. Then take this test to see how well you understand important truths you have studied.

In the right-hand margin write "True" or "False" after each of the following statements.

1. As Christians, we are to labor with God. _____

2. Attractive things can be made of wood, hay, and stubble. _____

3. Rewards are based on the quantity of work performed. _____

4. If a man's work is burned up, he shall be lost. _____

5. Some works of the unsaved may merit salvation. _____

6. A steward is to be found faithful. _____

7. The one who will judge us is the Lord Himself. _____

8. Christians can expect to be honored by this world. _____

9. It is the power of God that gives the Christian confidence. _____

10. The body of the Christian is the temple of the Holy Spirit. _____

Turn to page 64 and check your answers.

Discipline, Lawsuits, and Impurity

5:1—6:20

Discipline in the churches 5:1-13

Paul heard of a morals offense in the church, which condition continued. The indifference to such conditions was damaging to the testimony of Christ as well as to the testimony of any church.

1. What intolerable situation had been permitted to exist in the church at Corinth?

5:1 _____

The word *fornication* implies that illicit relations were existing.

2. Instead of bragging about their church, what should these people have been doing?

5:2 _____

3. What action should have been taken on the first discovery of these things?

5:2 _____

4. What did Paul feel should be the effect of the judgment of the assembled church in this case?

5:5 _____

In order to bring a man to the end of his willful ways, it is sometimes necessary for God to permit Satan to proceed with his designs up to a certain point (PSALM 109:6; 83:16; I TIMOTHY 1:20).

5. If Satan is permitted by God to inflict disease and death on this one, what would be the result in the day of the Lord Jesus?

5:5; compare 3:15 _____

6. What will happen to a believer who yields to sin repeatedly?

11:32; compare HEBREWS 12:8 _____

7. If moral indifference is tolerated in one direction in a church, what will happen to the moral character of the whole church?

5:6 _____

A church cannot maintain its enthusiasm for high spiritual standards when it tolerates within its own circle those who are lowering the standards.

8. What then should this church do about the matter?

5:7 _____

9. If another professing Christian is known to be impure, what should be done?

5:11 _____

10. While the judging of those outside the Body of Christ as to their sins must be left to God, what responsibility does the church have concerning offenders in its own midst?

5:12, 13 _____

Sin is a subtle thing and it is not always easy to place responsibility, but in Corinth the sin was open and flagrant and there was no excuse for not acting promptly to remove the reproach of the outside world.

Lawsuits between Christians 6:1-11

Having dealt with a moral offense, the apostle now moves to another problem within the church, that of a legal offense.

11. How does Paul describe the legal problem?

6:1; compare verse 6 _____

12. Describe the course our Lord prescribed for such disagreements.

MATTHEW 18:15-17 _____

Note that the matter is wholly between Christians. When lawlessness breaks out and the interests of society are at stake, there should be an appeal to the law. However, when private and personal interests alone are at stake, the Christian is either to submit the matter to arbitration among the brethren or suffer patiently.

13. In what judgments will the saints have part in the coming day?

6:2, 3 _____

14. If Christians are to have such high responsibility in the future, what should they presently be able to do?

6:4, 5 _____

15. As far as flagrant violations of the law are concerned—offenses that mark people as unregenerate—of what may we be sure?

6:9, 10 _____

16. However, what was supposedly true of those to whom Paul was writing?

6:11 _____

Impurity of Christians 6:12-20

Having discussed the prevalent legal problem, the apostle now deals with Christian liberty and impurity.

17. What general principle does the apostle give even though one may have certain bodily appetites.

6:12 _____

18. While a certain action may be lawful, what may be the effect of doing it?

6:12 _____

No Christian dares allow himself full latitude lest he become a slave to that which will hinder his testimony. Lawful things wrongly used rob many of their power.

19. How is the Christian to regard all his bodily energies?

6:15 _____

20. What is the readiest defense against the sin of fornication?

6:18; compare II TIMOTHY 2:22 _____

21. Why is this a sin that deeply undermines character?

6:18 _____

Sexual impurity institutes a relation which affects the sinner's personality. It undermines the whole life in the body and is a falsifying of the relations in which the man stands to God and to others.

22. Why is the gravity of this sin increased?

6:19 _____

23. What should be the Christian's purpose, even in his body?

6:20 _____

check-up time No. 4

You have just studied some important truths about discipline, lawsuits, and impurity of Christians. Review your study by rereading the questions and your written answers. If you are not sure of an answer, reread the Scripture portion given to see if you can find the answer. Then take this test to see how well you understand important truths you have studied.

In the right-hand margin write "True" or "False" after each of the following statements.

1. The sin of chapter 5 was known by only a few. ⎯⎯⎯⎯⎯⎯

2. The one having done this deed should have been removed from this assembly. ⎯⎯⎯⎯⎯⎯

3. Believers may sin repeatedly without ill-effects. ⎯⎯⎯⎯⎯⎯

4. A church should tolerate known sin in its midst. ⎯⎯⎯⎯⎯⎯

5. Those outside the church are judged by God. ⎯⎯⎯⎯⎯⎯

6. Believers should go to court against other Christians when private and personal interests are at stake. ⎯⎯⎯⎯⎯⎯

7. The saints will judge the world and angels. ⎯⎯⎯⎯⎯⎯

8. Christians have liberty to do all things without ill-effects. ⎯⎯⎯⎯⎯⎯

9. Believers are responsible to flee from fornication. ⎯⎯⎯⎯⎯⎯

10. The Christian should glorify God even in his body. ⎯⎯⎯⎯⎯⎯

Turn to page 64 and check your answers.

Marriage

7:1-40

Paul now passes to certain definite questions raised by the Corinthians dealing first with marriage.

The purpose of marriage 7:1-7

1. On what ground did Paul advise celibacy for some?

7:1; compare verse 35 _____

2. What was one reason he thought others should be married?

7:2 _____

It might seem that Paul here puts marriage on a low basis—"to avoid fornication." However, it must be remembered that fornication was very prevalent at Corinth, where it was not regarded as a serious sin. He would have no Christian run the risk of compromise along this line.

3. What other reason did Paul give for marriage?

EPHESIANS 5:31; compare GENESIS 2:24 _____

4. Who are to regulate the joys of the marital relationship?

7:3 _____

5. For what purpose may the demands of the sexual life be interrupted?

7:5 _____

Notice that verse 6 goes with verse 5, and thus this is an allowance and not a command.

24

The problems of the married 7:8-24

6. What teaching of Christ does Paul now cite?

7:10; compare MARK 10:9 _____

7. In the case of mixed marriages, what did Paul urge husbands and wives to do if possible?

7:12, 13 _____

8. In instances where one party had been converted since marriage, what hope might there be in patient continuance in the home?

7:14; compare I PETER 3:1 _____

The word for "sanctified" basically means "set apart." The unbelieving partner and children are in a position to be more easily reached for Christ. The word rendered "unclean" is simply the opposite of "set apart" and means "else were they not set apart." The salvation of the child does not depend on the salvation of the parents, but a child is at a great disadvantage when neither parent is a Christian.

9. Instead of worrying about ritual differences, what was to be the Christian's concern?

7:19 _____

10. When one becomes a Christian, what should his attitude be to the occupation to which he has been called?

7:20-22 _____

11. Why cannot the Christian be the mere slave of an employer?

7:23 _____

12. As Christians, with whom will we always abide?

7:24 _____

The problems of the unmarried 7:25-40

In this section, the apostle discusses the problems of the unmarried young (verses 25-35), of parents (verses 36-38), and of widows (verses 39, 40).

13. What is one reason Paul believed celibacy was desirable?

7:26 _____

The apostle is not drawing a contrast between good and bad, but rather between good and better. The issue here is the temporality of marriage versus the eternality of the work of God.

The words rendered "present distresses" have the idea of tribulation and persecution. Paul asks, "Why take on the added burden of married life when the Christian life is hard enough already?"

14. What was another reason Paul believed celibacy was desirable?

7:29 _____

15. What was yet another reason Paul believed celibacy was desirable?

7:32, 33; compare verse 35 _____

16. State the general principle the apostle lays down concerning temporal things, whether marriage or anything else?

7:31 _____

Grotius tells us that the word for "fashion" was one taken from the theater and means the shifting of scenes, revealing an altogether new appearance. The same scene may not face us tomorrow; therefore, we must not permit ourselves to become engrossed in worldly interests.

17. Apparently, how had Paul seen some promising male workers spoiled?

7:33 _____

18. How had some women workers shown themselves after marriage?

7:34 _____

It is not that married life cannot be so consecrated, but that it introduces new cares hard to endure in connection with the Lord's work (verse 35). Verses 36-38 have to do with the case of a father who was disturbed about the matter of permitting his virgin daughter to marry. Paul is speaking in relation to the marriage customs of the time and conditions existing at Corinth. The father is to do as he feels best for the daughter's security, whether he permits marriage or objects to it.

19. For how long is the wife bound to her husband?

7:39; compare ROMANS 7:2 _____

20. What may one do after the death of the marriage partner?

7:39 _____

21. Only to whom may a Christian be married after the death of the marriage partner?

7:39 _____

check-up time No. 5

You have just studied some important truths about marriage. Review your study by rereading the questions and your written answers. If you are not sure of an answer, reread the Scripture portion given to see if you can find the answer. Then take this test to see how well you understand important truths you have studied.

In the right-hand margin write "True" or "False" after each of the following statements.

1. One reason for marriage is that God has commanded some to marry. _____

2. Only the wife is to regulate the marital relationship. _____

3. After a marriage partner becomes saved, both partners should still try to live together. _____

4. The believer may lead his marriage partner to salvation by a consistent Christian testimony. _____

5. When at least one parent is a Christian, the child has a great advantage in coming to know Christ as Saviour. _____

6. When one becomes a Christian, he should immediately enter some Christian employment. _____

7. The Christian is to serve his employer above everything else. _____

8. Marriage was considered a temporal thing by the apostle Paul. _____

9. The Christian is to use but not to abuse the things of this world. _____

10. Marriage is dissolved only by the death of the marriage partner. _____

Turn to page 64 and check your answers.

Christian Liberty— Exhortation

8:1-13

Having discussed problems within the church and problems between believers, the apostle moves on to the problem of Christian liberty. This is the principle that governs what a Christian can and cannot do. Although the principle is applied to the customs of that day, it is for us today as well.

The principle stated 8:1-8

Portions of sacrificial animals used in heathen rituals were disposed of by the priests as they saw fit, and much of this meat turned up in the markets. Thus, Christians faced the problem of buying and eating that which was forbidden under the Old Testament law (NUMBERS 25:2; PSALM 106:28). Also, should Christians attend banquets where such meat was used, for the sake of promoting friendliness with heathen neighbors? Paul begins by saying, "We know that we are fully instructed." Thus they knew that idols were nothing, and therefore the meat offered to them was in no way affected.

1. What is the logical end of knowledge alone?

8:1 _____

2. What should this knowledge produce toward those less advanced in spiritual understanding?

8:1; compare I THESSALONIANS 5:11 _____

3. If such knowledge leads to self-conceit and unsympathetic impatience with those still in spiritual darkness, what is revealed?

8:2 _____

4. Who is the man who has really come to be known of God?

8:3 _____

The Christian who really loves God is never "puffed up" by spiritual knowledge but holds the truth in humility. The love that is to edify others must be poured out on God.

5. While an idol seems to be everything in the mind of a deluded person, what is it actually?

8:4; compare PSALM 115:4-8 _____

6. What does God say of all who make graven images?

ISAIAH 44:9 _____

7. For the Christian, how many Gods are there?

8:6; compare verse 4 _____

8. What does Paul say of the Father?

8:6; compare ROMANS 11:36 _____

9. What does Paul say of Christ?

8:6; compare COLOSSIANS 1:16 _____

Paul thus points out that God has made good meat, even idol meat (JAMES 1:17).

10. However, how did the knowledge of meat offered to a powerless idol affect some?

8:7 _____

11. How then does eating or not eating idol meat affect one's relationship to God?

8:8; compare ROMANS 14:6 _____

The principle applied 8:9-13

12. Even though a believer has freedom because of superior knowledge, what might be a consequence of this liberty?

8:9 _____

13. What might the weak brother do who views the liberty of the strong brother?

8:10 _____

14. What might be another consequence of exercising Christian liberty?

8:11 _____

15. What might be a consequence of the one who exercises Christian liberty?

8:12 _____

Paul is saying that one's liberty is sin when it leads another into license.

16. What then should we be willing to do for the sake of Christ even when the doing of it could work no spiritual injury to ourselves?

8:13 _____

The point is that living up to one's light is the germ out of which all true morality must spring. One gets more light only as he lives up to that which he has. There is little hope for one who continually violates his own knowledge of right. Remember that independent conscience is not authoritative; its verdicts often need correction by the Word and the Holy Spirit. Regard for another's conscience should never lead one to go against what he knows to be the truth. However, the charity taught by the gospel would urge us to the high-level Christian principle of having regard for the prejudices of the weak until they can be safely brought to a better understanding of salvation through grace. In summary: although a Christian may have liberty because of knowledge, he controls it because of love (8:1 compared with 8:13).

check-up time No. 6

You have just studied some important truths about the principle of Christian liberty. Review your study by rereading the questions and your written answers. If you are not sure of an answer, reread the Scripture portion given to see if you can find the answer. Then take this test to see how well you understand important truths you have studied.

In the right-hand margin write "True" or "False" after each of the following statements.

1. The logical end of knowledge is true humility. _____

2. The true purpose of knowledge should be to edify others. _____

3. Only a scholar can really be known of God. _____

4. Although idols may be great in the minds of some, they are actually powerless. _____

5. The knowledge of meat offered to a powerless idol affected some Corinthians. _____

6. The eating of idol meat affected the Corinthian Christian's relationship to God. _____

7. A consequence of Christian liberty may be a stumbling block to those who are weak. _____

8. Christian liberty may cause another to sin. _____

9. The Christian is to exercise his liberty at all costs. _____

10. Although a Christian may have liberty because of knowledge, he should control it because of love. _____

Turn to page 64 and check your answers.

Christian Liberty— Examples

9:1—10:33

Having discussed the principle of Christian liberty, the apostle gives examples from his own life and the life of Israel as to how this principle was applied.

Example of Paul   9:1-27

The first example is positive and enforces the appeal for the suspension of one's own rights for the sake of greater influence with the weak.

1. What qualifications did Paul have to be an apostle?

9:1 _____

2. What was Paul's underlying purpose in adopting stringent rules for himself?

PHILIPPIANS 3:8; compare II CORINTHIANS 5:13-15 _____

_____

3. Does God endorse complete independence for the Christian worker?

9:7 _____

4. State one reason why God would expect His servants to labor with provision for their needs.

9:9; compare I TIMOTHY 5:18 _____

Notice that although believers have the right to be supported by their ministry, their motive for work should not be "filthy lucre" (I PETER 5:2).

5. What could Paul have rightfully expected of these Corinthian believers?

9:11, 12 _____

6. Yet, because of the tendency of unbelievers to regard evangelists as engaged in the work for easy money, what had Paul been willing to do?

9:12; compare ACTS 20:33, 34 _____

7. What, then, did Paul consider his reward?

9:18 _____

Now that Paul has established his personal rights, he shows that he uses his rights in the interests of the gospel and his hearers.

8. While Paul was released by the gospel from slavery to men, why was he ready to become a voluntary servant of others without charge?

9:19 _____

9. Why was he ready to make concessions to the Jews, Gentiles, and weaker brothers when he could act without violation of Christian principles?

9:20-22 _____

But not only was there the motive of the gospel, there was also the motive of self-discipline as seen in 9:24-27.

10. For what purpose do runners run a race?

9:24 _____

11. What should a runner do to prepare himself for the race?

9:25 _____

12. Why did Paul seek to keep complete control over his bodily appetites at all times?

9:27 _____

The expression "keep under my body" is more literally, "I beat myself black and blue." The thought is that he wanted nothing to happen that should disqualify him for public service for Christ. The word for "castaway" actually means "disapproved" or "put on the shelf." Paul was not suggesting loss of salvation (9:26; compare II TIMOTHY 1:12) but the shame of being set aside because of some excess or inconsistency after having been used of God to win so many.

Example of Israel 10:1-33

Having used a positive example, Paul now recalls the failure of Israel. He thereby reminds them that Christian liberty does mean freedom from the Mosaic law system, but does not mean license to do anything. Israel once enjoyed a high privilege, but came under chastisement because of presuming upon God.

13. How many Israelites were identified with Moses and ate and drank of the same spiritual food?

10:2-4 _____

14. In spite of all these spiritual advantages, what happened to many Israelites because they did not believe their profession?

10:5 _____

15. Of what value is this for us?

10:6; compare verse 11 _____

16. What were some of their sins that we should avoid?

10:7-10 _____

17. What must every disobedient child of God expect?

Hebrews 12:5-7 _____

18. For what moment is Satan always watching?

10:12 _____

19. When temptation comes, why is it not necessary for the Christian to be defeated?

10:13 _____

20. What is always the way of escape?

Psalm 124:7, 8 _____

The better rendering of the last part of I Corinthians 10:13 is: "make *the* way of escape." This is not that the temptation will be removed, but that an escape will be made simultaneously with the temptation to encourage us. We must turn our faces in that direction.

21. What is the best defense against the sin of idolatry?

10:14 _____

The apostle next discusses consistency in relation to believers assembling at the Lord's table. Since this experience implies intimate fellowship with God's people, it is not fitting that those who have been partaking at heathen feasts should come directly to His table.

22. What is implied by taking the communion cup and bread?

10:17 _____

23. What would some think of Christians who attended heathen feasts, however meaningless the ceremonies might be to them?

10:20 _____

24. Should one who belongs to the fellowship of Christ's Body expose himself to demon religions?

10:21 _____

25. How was the Christian to regard meat purchased in the market even though it might be part of a sacrificed victim?

10:25, 26 _____

26. When might it be better not to eat idol meat?

10:28 _____

27. In regard to whose conscience may it be better to sacrifice a personal desire on some occasions?

10:29 _____

Verse 30 is literally, "If I partake with thankfulness, why should I be criticized or have to regard another's convictions?" Paul then shows that our action should still be governed by the Spirit of Christ and a willingness to help the weaker brother.

28. What should be the guiding principle in all our affairs?

10:31 _____

29. What was Paul always ready to sacrifice in order to attract souls to Christ?

10:33 _____

check-up time No. 7

You have just studied some important truths about the examples of Christian liberty. Review your study by rereading the questions and your written answers. If you are not sure of an answer, reread the Scripture portion given to see if you can find the answer. Then take this test to see how well you understand important truths you have studied.

In the right-hand margin write "True" or "False" after each of the following statements.

1. One qualification of an apostle was to have seen Christ. _____

2. Christian ministers have the right to be supported by their ministry. _____

3. Paul had been completely supported by the Corinthian believers. _____

4. Paul was commanded by God to become a servant of others without charge. _____

5. Paul made concessions without violation of Christian principles to win many to Christ. _____

6. Even the bodily appetites should be controlled to be an effectual servant of Christ. _____

7. The best defense against idolatry is to examine it carefully. _____

8. It is good for Christians to get as close as possible to demon religions. _____

9. Whatever a Christian does should be done to the glory of God. _____

10. Selfish desires should always be sacrificed that souls may be saved. _____

Turn to page 64 and check your answers.

Church Conduct

11:1-34

The attire of women   11:1-16

This section concerns behavior and decorum in public worship. The conduct of women involves the principle of subjection to the man. Paul's chief argument in this section has to do with "headship" (see verse 3). In the church the woman covers her head to acknowledge the headship of the man, and the man leaves his head uncovered to acknowledge the headship of Christ.

1. Who is the head of the man?

11:3; compare EPHESIANS 5:23 _____

2. Who is the head of the woman?

11:3; compare EPHESIANS 5:23, 24 _____

Notice that headship means subjection, not inferiority.

3. If a woman did not cover her head, what would she be doing?

11:5 _____

4. At what particular times was a woman to have her head covered or be veiled?

11:5 _____

5. What is one reason why the woman is subject to man?

11:7-9; compare GENESIS 2:22 _____

6. What other group of beings are evidently taught from this relationship?

11:10; compare I PETER 1:12 _____

7. To whom are all things subject?

11:12 _____

Verse 13, according to many writers, should not read as a question but as a simple statement. The change from question to statement does not involve a change in the order of words in Greek, as in English, but the context must decide. Here the meaning is: "Judge in yourselves (by what Paul has answered) that it is proper for a woman to pray to God unveiled."

8. Were Paul's instructions to the Corinthians intended to be localized and confined to them?

1:2 _____

9. Was it the custom in the early church to be contentious about apostolic teaching?

11:16 _____

The apostle therefore concludes that recognition of subjection is more important than the sign of that subjection.

The Lord's Supper 11:17-34

Paul passes to a second point of order in the assemblies, that of conduct at the Lord's table.

10. What was responsible for certain unscriptural practices concerning the Lord's Supper?

11:18 _____

The word for "heresies" in verse 19 means "sects" or "factions" (ACTS 5:17; 26:5).

11. What else was to be avoided at the Lord's Supper?

11:20-22 _____

12. What was Paul's opinion of those who did such a thing?

11:22 _____

13. At what time of day was the first Lord's Supper held?

11:23 _____

14. Which element did our Lord introduce first?

11:23 _____

15. For what reason did Christ ask them to observe this supper?

11:24 _____

16. How many times was the sacrifice of Christ to be repeated?

HEBREWS 10:10-12 _____

Notice then that this sacrifice was not to be repeated, but rather to be remembered.

17. What element did our Lord take next?

11:25 _____

18. For how long is the memorial table to be observed in the church?

11:26 _____

The word *show* means "preach." It is a public profession that the Lord has died once for all as an atoning sacrifice for us, that He now lives on our behalf, and that He is coming again as He said.

19. If people desecrate this solemn ordinance, how would they be considered?

11:27 _____

The expression "shall be guilty of" means, "will be liable for" or "have to answer for." They would be guilty of killing Christ as a criminal. Thus, for them Christ would not be regarded as the atoning Saviour.

20. What should one do before coming to the Lord's table?

11:28 _____

The expression "eateth and drinketh damnation" (verse 29) is more correctly rendered, "passes sentence upon himself." This one contracts for chastisement (verses 30-32).

21. How may God deal with those who trifle with spiritual realities?

11:30 _____

Compare the word *sleep* here with its use in 15:51.

22. If a believer will by the Holy Spirit's help examine and confess his own sin (I JOHN 1:9), what may be avoided?

11:31 _____

23. What is one reason the Lord chastens believers?

11:32; compare HEBREWS 12:5-8 _____

24. What was the final decision regarding the plan of combining the Lord's table with a church supper?

11:34 _____

check-up time No. 8

You have just studied some important truths about conduct in the church. Review your study by re-reading the questions and your written answers. If you are not sure of an answer, reread the Scripture portion given to see if you can find the answer. Then take this test to see how well you understand important truths you have studied.

In the right-hand margin write "True" or "False" after each of the following statements.

1. The man is the head of the woman.   _____

2. The woman was to signifiy her subjection to the man even when worshiping God.   _____

3. One reason woman is subject to man is because God made man and woman in this order.   _____

4. Angels must cover their heads when they pray to God.   _____

5. All things are subject to man.   _____

6. There was great unity in the Corinthian church at the Lord's table.   _____

7. It was proper to eat a meal at the Corinthian church when partaking of the Lord's Supper.   _____

8. The reason for the ordinance of the Lord's Supper is to remember His death until He comes again.   _____

9. One should carefully examine his own spiritual life before partaking of the Lord's Supper.   _____

10. One should examine his life and confess his sin that God might not have to chasten him.   _____

Turn to page 64 and check your answers.

The Christian and Gifts

12:1-31

Paul now comes to the discussion of spiritual gifts. In the church there are persons endowed with a variety of special services. Not all can serve in the same way; but whatever one's gift, it is to be used for the edification of all or it is being misused.

1. Before some of these people had become Christians, how were their gifts controlled?

12:2 _____

2. Who alone controls the gifts of Christians?

12:3 _____

It is recorded that strange things happened in some of the early churches. Members carried away by what they called the Divine Spirit, actually denied the deity of Christ.

3. What is the special ministry of the Holy Spirit?

JOHN 15:26 _____

The unity of the gifts   12:4-11

4. While there are essential differences in our lives and capabilities, what produces essential unity which at once combines and utilizes the variety of gifts?

12:4, 5 _____

44

5. Although it is the same God who works in each life, how does He work?

12:6 _____

6. For what purpose are the gifts of the Holy Spirit given?

12:7 _____

7. What *intellectual* gifts are utilized by the Spirit?

12:8 _____

Weiss says, "The word *wisdom* belongs to the sphere of teaching. In *knowledge*, on the other hand, the thought is limited to the apprehension of truth."

8. What *miraculous* gifts may God be pleased to bestow for His special purposes?

12:9, 10 _____

There is no one method of healing nor is there evidence that the kind of healings performed by our Lord and His apostles are to be continued throughout this age. God gives special skill to various types of healers, and remedies provided in nature were put there by Him for man's use. Paul's companion who ministered often to him was Luke, the physician.

9. For what purpose did God permit certain ones to perform miracles in the days when the church was taking root in the world?

ROMANS 15:19; compare HEBREWS 2:3, 4 _____

_____

10. Before His ascension, what had our Lord said concerning "prophecy"?

JOHN 16:13 _____

11. What might be said of some who prophesy?

I John 4:1 _____

12. What will always accompany a genuine gift of tongues imparted by the Holy Spirit?

14:27 _____

13. What did Paul say about the free exercise of this gift?

14:19 _____

14. Who energizes the believer in the exercise of his gifts?

12:11 _____

Gifts of the Spirit transcend the gifts of nature but function through our sanctified human talents. He quickens our dormant faculties, reinforces our capabilities, does away with ineffectiveness, banishes fear. He gives to the mind new powers of perception. Too often Christians who are naturally gifted for special work are lacking in spiritual power and are therefore ineffective.

The diversity of the gifts 12:12-31

15. Which basic ministry of the Spirit of God has been experienced by all Christians?

12:13 _____

16. What ministry of the Holy Spirit did Christ say would come at Pentecost?

Acts 1:5 _____

17. Which ministry of the Holy Spirit did Peter say had come at Pentecost?

Acts 11:15, 16 _____

The Pentecostal baptism had to do with the formation into one spiritual body all those who had believed in the Lord Jesus (ACTS 2:41, 47). Paul now speaks of this baptism in the past tense, for henceforth each by faith becomes united by the Spirit to the Body of Christ, which is that baptism.

18. What analogy does Paul make to emphasize that each believer with his spiritual gift contributes to the beauty of the whole spiritual structure?

12:14-16 _____

19. Why should not all believers have the same gift?

12:17-19 _____

20. How important is it for the whole body to be functioning?

12:21-23 _____

21. What should be our principal care if the whole body is to be kept functioning?

12:25 _____

22. What may we legitimately covet?

12:31 _____

check-up time No. 9

You have just studied some important truths about the Christian and spiritual gifts. Review your study by rereading the questions and your written answers. If you are not sure of an answer, reread the Scripture portion given to see if you can find the answer. Then take this test to see how well you understand important truths you have studied.

In the right-hand margin write "True" or "False" after each of the following statements.

1. The gifts of Christians are controlled by the Holy Spirit. _____

2. God gives the same gifts to all believers. _____

3. Spiritual gifts are given for the profit of all Christians. _____

4. Both wisdom and knowledge are spiritual gifts. _____

5. All who prophesy must evidently have the gift of prophecy. _____

6. The gift of tongues must always be accompanied by an interpreter. _____

7. All Christians are baptized by the Holy Spirit when they believe. _____

8. Some spiritual gifts are more necessary than others. _____

9. Believers should care for their own gifts, not for those of others. _____

10. The best spiritual gifts may be legitimately coveted. _____

Turn to page 64 and check your answers.

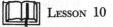

The Christian and Love

13:1-13

This chapter has been called "The Encyclopedia of Love." The English word *charity* used throughout does not express the original Greek word *agape*. *Agape* means "to love expecting nothing in return" and has its source in God alone (I JOHN 4:8). It is never found in the Greek classics.

In the ministry of spiritual gifts, it is love that edifies. Depth is to be preferred above diction. Love is the greatest thing, and gifts apart from love do not edify.

The pre-eminence of love   13:1-3

1. What happens if one has the gift of tongues but not love?

13:1 _____

2. Though one may have the most highly esteemed gifts, what is God's estimate of him when he is without heavenly love?

13:2 _____

3. What would happen to the most philanthropic person without this type of love?

13:3 _____

4. What would happen to one who is martyred for a great cause without this type of love?

13:3 _____

The properties of love   13:4-7

5. List some of the properties of divine love?

13:4 _____

_____

6. What further good properties are manifested by this type of love?

13:5 _____

_____

7. In what does one rejoice when controlled by this love?

13:6 _____

8. Describe other good qualities this love brings out in one's character.

13:7 _____

The word for "beareth" has the meaning of "over-roofing" or "covering" (MARK 2:4). "Believeth all things" means "is disposed to believe the best possible," not always putting the most unpleasant possible construction on everything done by others. The word for "endureth" is not the same thought as "beareth," but means "stands its ground almost to the breaking point."

The permanence of love   13:8-13

9. What happens to some of the gifts that will not happen to love?

13:8 _____

10. What is true of our knowledge now?

13:9 _____

11. Why is it important that we constantly recognize our present limitations and therefore be truly humble?

13:9-12 _____

It is certain that when we see all things clearly in heaven's light, we will regret that we cherished and bitterly fought for many ideas which were of no great importance in God's sight (verse 11).

12. As Paul, in concluding his treatise on love, includes all three elements of man's personal activity in his relation to God, which element does he say must hold the place of supremacy as that which binds our hearts to God?

13:13 _____

God is love. When we love with that divine love which the Holy Spirit sheds abroad in our hearts, His life is manifested in us. No gift can properly function apart from this.

check-up time No. 10

You have just studied some important truths about divine love. Review your study by rereading the questions and your written answers. If you are not sure of an answer, reread the Scripture portion given to see if you can find the answer. Then take this test to see how well you understand important truths you have studied.

In the right-hand margin write "True" or "False" after each of the following statements.

1. Spiritual gifts without love edify the saints. _____

2. Philanthropy without divine love is of great profit. _____

3. A martyrdom for a great cause without divine love is worthless. _____

4. People who truly love others sometimes become conceited about it. _____

5. When controlled by divine love, one will rejoice in truth. _____

6. Some spiritual gifts were temporary. _____

7. Divine love is a temporary thing. _____

8. In our present life we have only partial knowledge. _____

9. We will consider the same things important in heaven that we consider important now. _____

10. The greatest thing of all is divine love. _____

Turn to page 64 and check your answers.

Prophecy and Tongues

14:1-40

It is significant that only in Corinth, the center of Greek religious influence, did the manifestation known as "unknown tongues" attain so great a degree of prominence as to call for rigid rules from the apostle Paul. Any person who carefully studies this chapter will go slow in seeking the gift of unknown tongues.

That there may be a genuine spiritual gift of tongues is not denied, but where it is of the Holy Spirit its manifestation will be in strict accord with the inspired regulations found in this chapter. Bear in mind that similiar manifestations are witnessed in connection with heathen religions.

Wise is the Christian who allows the Spirit to work as *He* wills. Those who make one particular religious experience of primary importance are in danger of being deceived by spirits of a dangerous kind, particularly when they follow the directions of leaders who tell them to let their minds "go blank." There are human bodies that are especially susceptible to unseen powers, the nature of which one cannot always discern.

1. What gift did Paul consider more important than tongues?

14:1 _____

The Greek word means "forth-telling" or preaching, proclaiming the truth, not prediction.

2. If one is going to preach, to what purpose should it be?

14:3 _____

3. What happens when one speaks in an unknown tongue?

14:4 _____

53

4. How does Paul evaluate tongues as compared with plain speaking?

14:5 _____

5. To what extent does speaking in tongues prepare one for effectual service?

14:8 _____

6. What does speaking in tongues lack?

14:9 _____

7. How much understanding is there for the one who hears another speaking in tongues?

14:11 _____

8. Give one aim of those speaking in the church.

14:12 _____

9. What happens to the listener when he does not understand the giving of thanks?

14:17 _____

10. What is Paul's plain conclusion?

14:19 _____

11. What may be the effect on unsaved persons who are present when one is speaking in tongues?

14:23 _____

12. What is the general principle for anything done in God's house?

14:26 _____

13. If the tongues manifestation is of God, what is the maximum number to speak at any one meeting?

14:27 _____

14. How is one of these listeners to respond?

14:27 _____

15. What is one to do about speaking in tongues unless he is sure someone is going to interpret what he says?

14:28 _____

16. Who may prophesy (forth-tell) in the church as long as only one speaks at a time?

14:31 _____

17. Of what is God not the author?

14:33 _____

18. Although women may have the gift, by what principle should they abide when there is authority in the assembly?

14:34 _____

19. What gift should one seek?

14:39 _____

20. How should all things, even the work of the church, be done?

14:40 _____

check-up time No. 11

You have just studied some important truths about the gifts of preaching and speaking in tongues. Review your study by rereading the questions and your written answers. If you are not sure of an answer, reread the Scripture portion given to see if you can find the answer. Then take this test to see how well you understand important truths you have studied.

In the right-hand margin write "True" or "False" after each of the following statements.

1. The spiritual gift of tongues was as important as any other spiritual gift. _____

2. One purpose of preaching is for edification. _____

3. Speaking in tongues edifies the whole church. _____

4. Speaking in tongues lacks the understanding of the saints. _____

5. According to Paul, speaking with understanding is more important than speaking in tongues. _____

6. When one speaks in tongues, another should interpret. _____

7. If there is no one in the church to interpret one may speak in tongues anyway. _____

8. God may use confusion in the church for the edification of the saints. _____

9. When there is authority in the assembly, women should remain silent. _____

10. All things should be done decently and in order. _____

Turn to page 64 and check your answers.

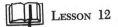

Resurrection, Collection, and Conclusion

15:1—16:24

The question of the resurrection had been raised at Corinth. Apparently there were traces of Sadducean doctrine (MATTHEW 22:23) among the Jews, and the Athenian doctrine (ACTS 17:32) among the Gentiles. Materialistic conceptions of the resurrection of the body had led to the adoption of the view that there was no resurrection properly so-called, but only a survival of the soul after death, or possibly a resurrection out of a life of sin into a life of righteousness. Paul meets these errors by insisting on the bodily resurrection of Jesus as a fundamental fact on which the whole gospel rests.

The certainty of the resurrection 15:1-34

1. What three great facts are made basic to the gospel?

15:3, 4 _____

_____

2. Who of the twelve disciples had the first glimpse of the resurrected Lord?

15:5; compare LUKE 24:34 (Compare JOHN 1:40-42 to resolve the

difference in the names.) _____

3. What was the largest number of believers who saw the risen Lord at one time?

15:6 _____

4. When did Paul see the risen Lord?

ACTS 9:5; compare 15:8 _____

5. To what is our resurrection related?

15:13 _____

6. To what does gospel preaching amount if we have only a dead Christ?

15:14 _____

7. If the bodily resurrection was not a fact, in what kind of position would this place the apostles?

15:15 _____

8. What would happen to our sins if Christ were not risen?

15:17 _____

9. What then would happen to those who die in Christ?

15:18 _____

10. What would happen if we had hope for this present life only?

15:19 _____

11. What is our guarantee that salvation includes the whole man, material as well as immaterial?

15:20 _____

12. How is Christ's resurrection described in the order of resurrection?

15:23 _____

Notice the two distinct kinds of resurrection (JOHN 5:29). There is no basis for any assumption that "they that are Christ's" includes all mankind (PHILLIPPIANS 3:18-21).

13. What kind of resurrection will the unsaved have in their time?

JOHN 5:29 _____

14. How many years will lie between the first and final resurrections?

REVELATION 20:4-6 _____

Verse 29 is translated by Sir Robert Anderson: "Else what shall become of them which are being baptized. It is for corpses if the dead rise not." Water baptism sets forth entombment in death and being raised in newness of life (ROMANS 6:3, 4). But if there is no resurrection, baptism is for the sake of the absolutely dead. Well may we ask, Why baptize in this manner if Jesus was never raised? The rite loses its meaning. Baptism is brought in to show that Christ's resurrection is vital to God's truth in every way.

The program of the resurrection   15:35-58

15. What must happen to a natural seed before it can spring up and bear fruit?

15:36 _____

16. How do celestial and terrestrial bodies differ?

15:42-44 _____

17. From whom do we derive our natural natures and bodies?

15:45 _____

18. What power has the last Adam (Christ) that the first Adam did not possess?

15:45 _____

19. How is the first man described?

15:47 _____

Verse 49 is more literally: "As we have borne the image of the earthly, let us bear the image of the heavenly." The idea seems to be that, by looking forward to our future glory, we let His resurrection glory be seen in us.

20. What is the mystery that will happen to *some* Christians?

15:51 _____

21. What will happen to *all* Christians?

15:51 _____

22. When are believers to receive the gift of immortality (a glorious, imperishable body) in addition to the already-possessed gift of eternal life?

15:52, 54 _____

23. What is the real seed of death?

15:56 _____

24. Who then has given us the victory over sin and death?

15:57 _____

25. What is the practical application of this important doctrine?

15:58 _____

The collection for the saints   16:1-4

It would appear that Paul's visit to Jerusalem and the character of his discussions there had suggested a fellowship fund on the part of the Gentile churches.

26. Which churches were already co-operating in the plan?

16:1 _____

27. For what special class in the churches did the apostles have great concern?

GALATIANS 2:10 _____

28. Toward what class of the poor does the church have a primary obligation?

GALATIANS 6:10 _____

29. When was the natural time for taking the fellowship offering?

16:2; compare ACTS 20:7 _____

30. How were they to determine how much to give?

16:2; II CORINTHIANS 8:12-15 _____

Conclusion 16:5-20

31. List five imperatives which might well adorn the lives of every Christian.

16:13, 14 _____

_____

You have just studied some important truths about the resurrection and the collection. Review your study by rereading the questions and your written answers. If you are not sure of an answer, reread the Scripture portion given to see if you can find the answer. Then take this test to see how well you understand important truths you have studied.

In the right-hand margin write "True" or "False" after each of the following statements.

1. Peter was the first disciple to view the resurrected Lord.   _____

2. The apostle Paul personally saw the resurrected Lord.   _____

3. If Christ were not risen, we could still be saved.   _____

4. Our resurrection depends on the resurrection of Christ.   _____

5. There are three distinct kinds of resurrection.   _____

6. Our resurrection body will be incorruptible.   _____

7. All Christians will die a physical death.   _____

8. Sin is the cause of physical death.   _____

9. An offering was to be taken once a month.   _____

10. Christians are to give to the Lord as He has prospered them.   _____

Turn to page 64 and check your answers.

Suggestions for class use

1. The class teacher may wish to tear this page from each workbook as the answer key is on the reverse side.

2. The teacher should study the lesson first, filling in the blanks in the workbook. He should be prepared to give help to the class on some of the harder places in the lesson. He should also take the self-check tests himself, check his answers with the answer key and look up any question answered incorrectly.

3. Class sessions can be supplemented by the teacher's giving a talk or leading a discussion on the subject to be studied. The class could then fill in the workbook together as a group, in teams, or individually. If so desired by the teacher, however, this could be done at home. The self-check tests can be done as homework by the class.

4. The self-check tests can be corrected at the beginning of each class session. A brief discussion of the answers can serve as review for the previous lesson.

5. The teacher should motivate and encourage his students. Some public recognition might well be given to class members who successfully complete this course.

answer key

to self-check tests

Be sure to look up any questions you answered incorrectly.

A gives the correct *answer*.

R *refers* you back to the number of the question in the lesson itself, where the correct answer is to be found.

Mark with an "x" your wrong answers.

	TEST 1		TEST 2		TEST 3		TEST 4		TEST 5		TEST 6	
Question	A	R	A	R	A	R	A	R	A	R	A	R
1	T	2	T	1	T	2	F	1	T	3	F	1
2	T	4	F	5	T	4	T	3	F	4	T	2
3	F	7	T	10	F	7	F	6	T	7	F	4
4	T	9	T	13	F	9	F	7	T	8	T	5
5	F	16	F	15	F	10	T	10	T	8	T	10
6	T	20	T	16	T	17	F	11	F	10	F	11
7	T	23	T	17	T	18	T	13	F	11	T	12
8	F	24	F	18	F	22	F	18	T	13	T	14
9	T	26	T	19	T	24	T	20	T	16	F	16
10	T	27	T	22	T	11	T	23	T	19	T	16

	TEST 7		TEST 8		TEST 9		TEST 10		TEST 11		TEST 12	
Question	A	R	A	R	A	R	A	R	A	R	A	R
1	T	1	T	2	T	2	F	2	F	1	T	2
2	T	4	T	4	F	5	F	3	T	2	T	4
3	F	6	T	5	T	6	T	4	F	3	F	8
4	F	8	F	6	T	7	F	5	T	6	T	9
5	T	9	F	7	F	11	T	7	T	10	F	12
6	T	12	F	10	T	12	T	9	T	14	T	16
7	F	21	F	12	T	15	F	9	F	15	F	20
8	F	24	T	15	F	20	T	10	F	17	T	23
9	T	28	T	20	F	21	F	11	T	18	F	29
10	T	29	T	22	T	22	T	12	T	20	T	30

how well did you do?

0-1 wrong answers—excellent work

2-3 wrong answers—review errors carefully

4 or more wrong answers—restudy the lesson before going on to the next one